Fiona
the
flower girl

By Carley Roney
& the editors of *the knot*

Illustrated by
Lorena Siminovich

chronicle books · san francisco

To Havana,
my favorite flower girl
—C. R.

♥

To Catalina,
for the inspiration
—L. S.

Text © 2008 by The Knot.
Illustrations © 2008 by Lorena Siminovich.

Design by Katie Jennings.
Typeset in Aged & Amelie.
The illustrations were rendered in digital collage.
Manufactured in China.

Library of Congress Cataloging-in-Publication Data
Roney, Carley.
Fiona the flower girl / by Carley Roney and the editors of The Knot ;
illustrated by Lorena Siminovich.
p. cm.
ISBN 978-0-8118-5903-5
1. Flower girls—Juvenile literature. 2. Wedding etiquette—Juvenile literature.
I. Siminovich, Lorena ill. II. Knot (Firm) III. Title.
BJ2065.W43R66 2008
395.2'2—dc22
2007000295

10 9 8 7 6 5 4 3 2 1

Chronicle Books LLC
680 Second Street, San Francisco, California 94107

www.chroniclekids.com

this book is for _____,

the flower girl in _____'s

wedding on _____

The summer when Fiona turned eight
was a very important summer. First,
she got a purple bicycle for her birthday
in June.

Then, in July, she went to the beach and
found 34 perfect shells and a starfish.

And just as the summer was ending,
another wonderful thing happened:
Fiona's Aunt Caroline got *engaged*.

When you get engaged, it means you're going to get *married*. Aunt Caroline had a ring to prove it, with a diamond that was sparkly and clear.

Fiona thought it would be much better to have a ring that was purple, but she could tell that Aunt Caroline was very happy with her clear ring.

Aunt Caroline was going to marry a
man named Brian. Fiona liked Brian.
He had a friendly smile, and he made
Aunt Caroline laugh a lot.
So Fiona approved.

Then came the big surprise: Aunt Caroline asked Fiona if she would be a *flower girl* in the wedding!

"What does that mean?" asked Fiona,
since she'd never been to a wedding before.

"It means you wear a pretty dress, and carry
a basket of flowers, and walk down the aisle
in front of me," Caroline explained.
"Does that sound good?"

"It's a *very special honor*,"
Fiona's mother said.

Fiona didn't have to think very long.

"Sure!" she said.

"Yay!" Aunt Caroline said, and she gave Fiona a big hug.

So it was official: Fiona was going to be a *flower girl*.

But the wedding was a long way away. It wasn't until next June, almost a whole year! Fiona could hardly believe it took so long to get ready for a wedding. She wondered if she would get tired of getting ready.

But actually, getting ready turned out to be *fun*!

The first fun thing was trying on the official flower-girl *dress*. Fiona went to the store with Aunt Caroline and her mom and tried on fancy dresses, some so long they touched the floor. They were like princess gowns!

Fiona was glad that she and Aunt Caroline both liked the same one best.

The next fun thing was the *shower*.
A shower is a party for the bride that
happens before the wedding. Fiona
thought "shower" was a weird name
for a party.

"It means we shower the bride with
gifts," Fiona's mom explained.

Fiona laughed, imagining people pouring
buckets of tiny presents on top of
Aunt Caroline.

But even though no one got to
pour any presents, Fiona *loved*
the party.

Only girls and ladies were invited,
and they ate coconut cake and drank
raspberry lemonade while Aunt Caroline
opened gifts.

The best part was that Aunt Caroline
really liked the purple teapot that Fiona
had picked out all by herself.

After the shower, Aunt Caroline had a surprise for Fiona: *a flower necklace*!

Fiona loved it—*especially* the purple petals! Aunt Caroline helped Fiona put the necklace on.

"You can wear this to remember your special part in my wedding," Aunt Caroline said. "I was a flower girl when I was your age, and it's one of my favorite *memories*. I hope you'll have a wonderful memory, too!"

"Thanks!" Fiona said.

"And thank you for being part of my big day!" Aunt Caroline said.

"You're welcome!" Fiona said.

If only the big day would hurry up and come!

And finally...after all the getting ready...it was time for the wedding!

First came the *rehearsal*, the night before the wedding. Fiona practiced walking down the aisle, just like she and her mom had practiced at home.

Then Fiona went home and got a good
night's sleep, because...

...the next day was the *wedding*!

Fiona loved putting on her dress and fixing her hair with a ribbon. She had never been so fancy in her whole life.

And she loved her flower-girl basket, which had pink and red rose petals inside.

Before the ceremony, Fiona waited with
the *bridesmaids*. They chatted about
weddings and laughed a lot. Fiona felt
like she was part of a very special club.

Then Fiona got to see Aunt Caroline
in her long white dress and Brian in
his fancy suit. They looked like movie
stars! The photographer snapped lots
of *pictures*.

After the photos, it was time to walk down the *aisle*. Fiona went right before Aunt Caroline, tossing petals as she walked. She smiled at her family in the audience, and they smiled back at her. There were smiles everywhere she looked!

Then, during the ceremony, Fiona got
to be right up close when Aunt Caroline
and Brian promised to love each other
for their whole lives. And then they
kissed and everyone clapped, Fiona too!

After the ceremony was over, it was time
for the *reception*. That was the best
part of the whole wedding, because Fiona
got to dance with Aunt Caroline and
her brand-new Uncle Brian. It was funny
calling him "uncle" now!

"You did a great job, Fiona," Aunt
Caroline said. "We're so proud of you!"

"Thanks," Fiona said, smiling her biggest
smile, because she was proud, too!

And then Fiona reached down and touched her necklace, and she made a wish—that she would always remember this very special day, when she was *Fiona the flower girl.*

a guide for parents of flower girls

Congratulations! Your daughter is going to be a flower girl. In addition to being the most adorable member of the bridal party, she—and you—have some pretty important responsibilities. If your daughter has never been to a wedding or doesn't know anyone who's ever been a flower girl, she probably doesn't understand exactly what's going on. She's bound to be excited once you tell her about her beautiful dress, the pretty flowers, and the importance of her job. So before you wonder, "What did I get myself into?" here's a breakdown of what you and your daughter need to know.

♥

the dress. Be prepared to pay for the dress—it's part of agreeing to be in the wedding. Prices vary depending on the designer, fabric, and size, but feel free to make some suggestions. A bride choosing on looks alone may overlook a scratchy collar or a heavy dress. Your daughter might have to go for fittings to make sure the dress is comfortable and not too long, to avoid tugging or tripping during the ceremony. Floor-length dresses can be tricky, especially if your daughter is younger or simply not used to walking in something so long. If you're worried, suggest shortening the hem by an inch or two.

the accessories. Here's a checklist you can use to make sure your flower girl has everything she needs for the big day:

♥ *shoes.* Often overlooked, shoes that don't fit will literally hurt your child's performance. Get them at least a month in advance, and have her break them in for a few hours each week (just around the house) to make sure she's comfortable. In a pinch, at a casual warm-weather wedding, you might suggest that she walk barefoot. It looks adorable!

♥ *jewelry.* Small pearl studs for pierced ears, or a simple bracelet, are perfect for the wedding day. It's best to keep the jewelry minimal—and make sure your daughter knows it's not the time to break out her favorite large, plastic ring.

♥ *white underwear.* Colors or polka dots easily show through a light dress, so white is the best bet.

♥ *stockings.* If your daughter will be wearing stockings, it's best to line up two pairs in case of wedding-day snags. And if the dress is white or ivory, make sure the stockings match—shades of white and ivory can be very different!

♥ *white cardigan.* If she gets cold, you don't want her to end up in a sweatshirt! A pretty cardigan to match her dress is great to have on hand.

♥ *hair accessories.* Will she wear barrettes, a tiara, or flowers in her hair? It's a good idea to check with the bride on this one, so you can line up the right supplies—especially if you're going to be your daughter's hairstylist.

practice makes perfect. Start "walking down the aisle" months before the wedding. The more confidence your daughter has, the more comfortable she'll be when it counts. If she's younger, try walking with her a few times, then have her show you how she can walk on her own. She should keep a steady pace that might seem slow at first—try having her count in her head, "one peanut butter, two peanut butter," with each step. Older flower girls should catch on pretty quickly, but it might take several practice sessions for the little ones to perfect their walk.

♥

the bridal shower. If your daughter is invited to the shower, be mindful of her attention span. Ask the host to recommend a good time for your daughter to arrive, and suggest giving her a special job at the party, like helping collect bows and ribbons to turn into the rehearsal bouquet. The bridal shower is a great opportunity for your daughter to meet the other members of the bridal party. Seeing friendly, familiar faces on the big day will help to ease any anxiety.

Beyond the shower, you might suggest the bride spend some one-on-one time with your daughter and let her know how excited she is to share her special day. Manicures or special shopping trips are great ways to bond!

hair and makeup. Is the bridal party getting fancy updos for the event? Ask if your daughter can go to the salon, too. Even if the stylist only brushes her hair and clips in a barrette or two, it will help her feel included. If your daughter is wearing a ring of flowers in her hair, make sure it's secure and won't fall over her eyes every few steps!

Try to minimize her time in the salon chair; if she has to sit still for two hours the morning of the wedding, it may be hard for her to focus on the more important parts of the day. If you choose not to have a professional do her hair, be prepared with a comb and light hairspray for styling and touch-ups. Also, if you're planning to schedule a haircut, make it a week or two before the wedding to avoid harsh bangs and choppy layers.

If the bride is having her makeup professionally done, decide beforehand if you'd like to include your daughter, but don't let the makeup artist get carried away. It's not a beauty pageant, so a touch of lip gloss and a little translucent powder or a light stroke of blush is plenty.

the rehearsal. On or around the night before the wedding, your daughter will participate in the rehearsal. She might be intimidated by the attention, but assure her it's going to be just as you practiced. Walk with her down the aisle once or twice if she's uncomfortable, and show her where you'll be during her big moment. Don't worry if the rehearsal doesn't go perfectly—often the most nervous flower girls at the rehearsal turn into the best performers when it counts. She may be invited to the rehearsal dinner, but don't be offended if she's not—it's better to save her energy and attention for the big day.

getting **ready**. It's probably best to keep your daughter out of her dress until she has eaten, gone to the bathroom, washed her hands, and finished any other potentially messy tasks. Explain her duties again, and have her show you how she plans to hold her flowers, basket, or pomander.

She'll definitely feel included once she's around other dressed-up members of the bridal party, so make sure she has pre-ceremony face time with the bride and her ladies. Try to keep her occupied until right before the ceremony starts. It's not the bride's or attendants' job to watch her until it's time to go. If you can't be with her, designate someone to hold on to an "emergency kit" full of (non-messy) snacks, water or light-colored juice, and a favorite coloring book.

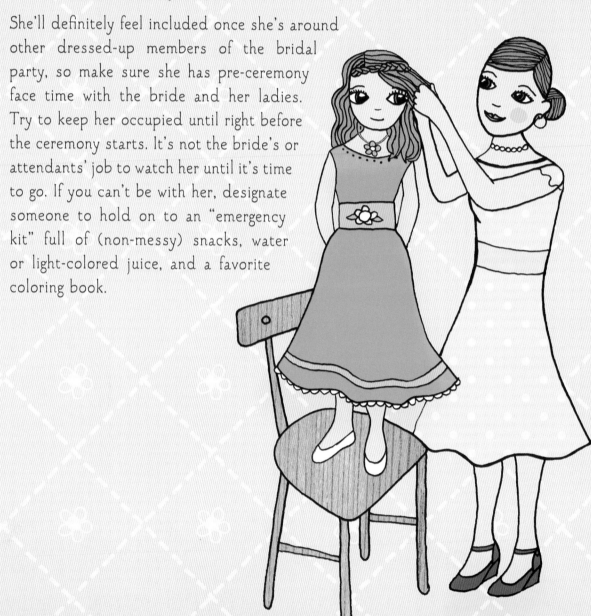

pomander

small bouquet

basket of flowers

the flowers. Flower girls don't necessarily toss petals; instead, she might hold a pomander (a ball of flowers suspended from a ribbon for her to clutch), a basket of flowers, or a mini-bouquet that matches the bride's.

Scattering a perfect blanket of petals is tricky, so if that's what the bride wants, someone should spread them before the ceremony. Then the flower girl can just sprinkle a few more petals on top. If the petals *won't* be spread beforehand, you may need to give your daughter a few petal-tossing pointers. Try a few practice steps while you explain how many petals to toss; otherwise, you could end up with a trail of single petals or a burst of petals at the beginning with none left over for the rest of the aisle. Have your daughter grasp three or four petals at a time (like gently picking up a handful of cotton balls) and drop them with each step.

Also, make sure the basket isn't too heavy for your daughter to carry, especially if she's young!

photos. Depending on whether your daughter loves to be in the limelight, it may or may not be hard for her to patiently endure a drawn-out photo session. You can stay with her while the photographer's snapping away, unless she's comfortable with the bridal party and old enough to handle it on her own. Explain the photo process to her before the wedding so she knows what to expect, and encourage her to show her prettiest smile (not the forced version that might appear after too many camera snaps), even if she's tired. Tell her you can't wait to see how beautiful the pictures will look after it's all over!

the walk. If she's younger than four (or very shy), walking down the aisle is probably the most worrisome part of the day for your little flower girl. Try to sit near the front of the audience next to the aisle; that way she'll be able to see you in case you need to (discreetly) coax her down the aisle. If you're in the wedding party, designate someone else to be your daughter's front-row helper, and make sure your daughter knows to look for that person if she gets nervous. Try bringing your daughter's favorite stuffed animal and keeping it with you up front where she can see it. If you worry that she might not make it all the way down the aisle, suggest that she walk before the maid of honor instead of before the bride. That way, if your daughter stalls or gets nervous, the maid of honor can guide her down the aisle.

If your daughter is older, she probably won't have a problem making it to the front of the ceremony, but make sure you practice her pace. All the excitement might cause her to rush—don't forget the "peanut butter" practice sessions!

standing still. Even the shortest ceremony will seem long to a young flower girl. If you think she might get fidgety, suggest that she sit with you after her walk down the aisle. Don't get caught up in making sure she acts perfectly; brides, grooms, and guests love the sweet innocence of child attendants. If, at any point, she throws a tantrum and you can't calm her down, it's better to get up and leave with her than to have guests watching you try to control her.

As soon as the ceremony is finished, quietly congratulate your daughter on a job well done!

the reception. Your daughter will probably be seated with you for the reception, not with the rest of the bridal party. Guests love to fuss over flower girls, but if she looks uncomfortable, feel free to step in and say, "We're happy that you think she did such a great job; she's had a busy and exciting day." They'll probably take the hint.

Typically, younger girls will last an hour or two at the reception, depending on what time it starts. For an evening reception, if you'd like to stay the whole night, arrange for a sitter to pick up your daughter. If she's older, encourage her to kick back and enjoy the party—and you should, too!

after it's all over. Talk about the big day with your flower girl, and make sure she has some photos so she can look back on the experience as she grows older. A special day like this will hopefully become a very clear childhood memory for her, one that she'll enjoy for years to come.

With best wishes,

Carley Roney and the editors of **the knot**

P.S. For more flower-girl advice and information, visit www.theknot.com/flowergirls.

- -

about the author

Carley Roney is the editor-in-chief and cofounder of **the knot**, the trusted source for wedding advice at www.theknot.com. She vividly remembers being a flower girl when she was five, wearing a pink and green satiny dress and dancing with the big girls at her dad's secretary's wedding!